DEPARTMENT OF THE NAVY
HEADQUARTERS UNITED STATES MARINE CORPS
2 NAVY ANNEX
WASHINGTON, DC 20380-1775

MARINE CORPS POLICY CONCERNING PREGNANCY AND PARENTHOOD

MCO 5000.12E
MPO-40
08 DEC 04

MARINE CORPS ORDER 5000.12E W/CH 1-2

From: Commandant of the Marine Corps
To: Distribution List

Subj: MARINE CORPS POLICY CONCERNING PREGNANCY AND PARENTHOOD

Ref: (a) SECNAVINST 1000.10
       (b) MCO P6100.12
       (c) MCO 1740.13A
       (d) MCO 1510.25C
       (e) MCO 1700.24B
       (f) MCO P11000.22
       (g) BUMEDINST 6320.3B
       (h) MCO P1080.40C
       (i) MCO P3000.13
       (j) NEHC-6260-TM-01, Reproductive/Developmental Hazards
       (k) MCO P1300.8R
       (l) OPNAVINST 6000.1B
       (m) OPNAVINST 3710.7T
       (n) BUMEDINST 6320.72
       (o) MCO P1040.31H
       (p) MCO 1001.45G
       (q) MCO P1900.16F
       (r) MCO P1040R.35
       (s) MCO P1050.3H
       (t) MCO P1020.34G
       (u) MCO P10120.28F

Encl: (1) Format for Commanding Officer Notification
       (2) Health Care Provider Pregnancy Notification to
           Commanding Officer/Officer in Charge (CO/OIC)
       (3) NAVMED 6260/9 (07-03), Occupational Exposures of
           Reproductive or Developmental Concern-Worker's
           Statement
       (4) NAVMED 6260/8 (07-03), Occupational Exposures of
           Reproductive or Developmental Concern - Supervisor's
           Statement

1. Purpose. To revise Marine Corps policy and procedures for pregnant
Marines and naval personnel (hereafter identified as servicewomen) assigned
to Marine units regarding the assignment, retention, separation, prescribed
standards of conduct, and medical management of normal pregnancies per
references (a) through (u). This policy also pertains to Marines considering
the adoption of an infant/child and single male parent Marines. For the
purpose of this Order, the procedures for Active Duty (AD) personnel are the
same for Active Reservist (AR).

2. Cancellation. MCO 5000.12D.

3. Information

    a. As indicated in reference (a), pregnancy is a natural event that can occur in the lives of Marines and Sailors, and can be compatible with a successful naval career. There are responsibilities that come with parenthood, and for those in uniform, these responsibilities require increased consideration and planning due to military commitments. Marines are expected to balance the demands of a naval career with their family plans and responsibilities.

    b. The overriding concern for commanding officers (COs), supervisory personnel, and health care providers responsible for pregnant servicewomen serving with the Marine Corps is to provide for the health and safety of the servicewoman and her unborn child while maintaining optimum job and career performance. Policy and procedures are required to ensure the health, welfare, and administrative support of pregnant Marines and Sailors, and to minimize the impact a pregnancy has on operational readiness.

    c. If a Marine is pregnant, they are non-deployable. For the purpose of this Order, a deployment is a contingency operation, an expeditionary operation, or a normal peacetime (6 or more months) operation.

    d. The decisions surrounding parenthood and family matters can best be made in an environment of concerned leadership. Military responsibilities require command attention to help Marines fulfill their duty to their unit and also meet family responsibilities.

    e. Pregnancy should not restrict tasks normally assigned to servicewomen, but may temporarily limit the ability to perform routine tasks associated with their current military occupational specialty (MOS) and/or billet, and may require temporary reassignment.

4. Responsibilities

    a. Individual Responsibilities

        (1) It is strongly recommended that the servicewoman make every effort to plan her pregnancy to enable her to successfully balance the demands of family responsibilities and military obligations. Normally, she will not be reassigned on the basis of pregnancy.

        (2) In order to allow commanders the opportunity to solidify and maintain unit integrity throughout a deployment life cycle, all servicewomen assigned to deploying units or units already deployed, will report to the medical department for pregnancy testing no earlier than (NET) 14 and no later than (NLT) 10 days prior to deployment. A urine pregnancy test is sufficient for verification. Marines who have undergone hysterectomy or bilateral tubal ligation are exempt.

        (3) During normal peacetime training and all other circumstances, the servicewoman shall seek confirmation of pregnancy by a military health care provider (HCP) or civilian HCP in cases of inaccessibility to a military treatment facility (MTF). She should also report as soon as possible to the supporting MTF to establish a prenatal care program.

        (4) The servicewoman is to notify her CO or Officer In Charge (OIC) regarding her pregnancy (enclosure (1)) as soon as possible, but no later

than two weeks after diagnosis of pregnancy. This will facilitate planning a request for replacement, if the servicewoman is in a seagoing/deployable billet.

(5) The servicewoman is responsible for performing military duties within the limits established by her pregnancy. She is also responsible for complying with work site and task related safety and health recommendations made by appropriate occupational health professionals, including the use of personal protective equipment.

(6) After delivery, servicewomen will participate in an exercise program, as soon as medically authorized, to prepare for the physical fitness test (PFT). No later than 6 months after being returned to full duty by the HCP, the servicewoman is required to take the PFT and conform to the acceptable height/weight standards per reference (b). Additional time may be recommended by HCP and granted, if necessary, due to unique medical circumstances.

b. Family Care Plan

(1) Any Marine anticipating the responsibilities associated with parenthood is required to make arrangements for child care to cover regular working hours, duty, exercises, war, and combat contingency deployment. This applies to Marine reservists on active duty/inactive duty for training (ADT/IDT) and upon being mobilized.

(2) All single servicemembers and dual military couples with eligible family members are responsible for initiating a formalized family care plan per reference (c). A completed family care plan will certify that family members will be cared for during the Marine's absence. It will also identify the designated legal guardian of the eligible family member(s), as well as the logistical, relocation, and financial arrangements.

(3) Marines are advised to contact their local Marine Corps Community Service (MCCS) Marine and Family Services programs center and legal assistance office for help in developing a family care plan. The Marine may complete a DD 2606, Request for Child Care Record, to place the newborn child or soon to be adopted child on the waiting list for childcare. This form is available online through the following website: http://www.dior.whs.mil/forms/DD2606.PDF.

c. Education of Marines

(1) The Marine Corps will provide education on the policies contained in this Order to all Marines, male and female, upon initial entry, and throughout their service in the Marine Corps to stress the importance of family planning and the responsibilities of parenthood.

(2) Per reference (d), COs will provide appropriate training as part of their units' orientation and annual troop information programs to ensure that all Marines are aware of the contents of this Order, and the broad range of medical, legal, financial, religious, and other services available to assist and encourage all Marines in making family life decisions that are supportive of both service obligations and their parental responsibilities.

(3) Per reference (e), appropriate family life education and counseling will be made available at MCCS centers throughout the Marine Corps to assist those who seek it in planning for and carrying out the responsibilities of parenthood.

(a) Marines will be afforded the opportunity to take advantage of available legal assistance for advice regarding their options in establishing paternity or seeking child support.

(b) Staff at the MCCSs, MTFs, and chaplains are available to provide counseling in preparation for pregnancy and parenthood, and give ongoing support and counseling for families to help them meet the requirements of the workplace and home. Services such as the New Parent Support Program, MCCS, child development programs, marriage preparation workshops, and personal financial management classes are available. Participation in these and similar programs should be highly encouraged for all Marines facing the challenges of parenthood.

d. Billeting

(1) Per reference (a), a pregnant active duty servicewoman with no family members may reside in bachelor quarters for her full term. If the pregnant servicewomen requests, the host commander may authorize her to occupy off-base housing up to her 20th week of pregnancy. From the 20th week onward, the host commander must approve a request to occupy off-base housing.

(2) Per reference (f), single pregnant servicewomen may request government housing, based on availability, before the birth of the child. However, they will not be authorized to move in to housing until after the birth of the child. However, they will not be given special treatment (i.e., head of line privilege on the base housing list). These policies allow single pregnant servicewomen to have their name on the housing list without waiting for the birth of the baby.

(3) Payment of basic housing allowance (BAH) will be per applicable pay and entitlement regulations. All approvals for allowances will be filed in the service record book (SRB)/officer qualification record (OQR) until such time as the approved Navy/Marine Corps (NAVMC) 10922 dependency application is completed, or the member is no longer entitled to BAH. Upon removal, the approval is retired to the command's correspondence files.

5. Notification Procedures

a. All pregnant servicewomen and Marines of either gender adopting a child, regardless of component/grade (except Individual Ready Reserve (IRR) and Standby Reserve Marines), will notify their commanding officer/ Commanding General, Marine Corps Mobilization Command (MOBCOM) (the latter by Individual Mobilization Augmentee (IMA) personnel only) in writing within 2 weeks of medical confirmation of pregnancy or 1 month prior to obtaining legal custody of the adopted child. The notification letter will be formatted per enclosure (1).

b. A copy of the notification letter will be retained in the Marine's SRB/OQR until the completion of the deployment deferment period (see paragraph 8d). Per enclosure (1), notification shall include the following:

(1) A statement that the service member understands the requirement to make arrangements for child care to cover regular working hours, duty, exercises, war, and combat contingency deployment. This applies to Marine reservists on ADT/IDT and Marines in the Selected Marine Corps Reserve (SMCR) upon being mobilized.

(2) In the case of servicewomen in the active component, active Reserve (AR), or a Reserve Marine on extended active duty (EAD), a statement that conveys the understanding that she remains eligible for reenlistment and will serve on active duty until the expiration of her active service obligation is required. A SMCR Marine will provide a statement that conveys that she will remain in the SMCR or request transfer to the IRR as applicable according to paragraph 18a.

(3) A statement of understanding that the servicewoman may request separation. In the case of pregnancy, she may remain eligible for medical care in limited circumstances per reference (g). The medical care will include prenatal, delivery, and postnatal care at an MTF, applicable to active component/AR Marines only. If the servicewoman feels that extenuating circumstances exist which preclude further service, the notification should include a request for separation per paragraph 18 of this Order. The request for separation may be submitted after the initial notification. In the case of the SMCR member, when retention is deemed medically inadvisable, transfer to the IRR to satisfy the term of service for which the servicewoman is obligated is authorized.

(4) A statement that the servicewoman/Marine understands she/he will be available for worldwide assignment and that there is no guarantee of special consideration in duty assignments or duty stations based solely on her pregnancy or the fact that she/he will have an eligible family member, except as provided for in this Order. This statement is not applicable to a SMCR servicewoman.

(5) A statement that the servicewoman/adopting Marine is aware of the limitations of eligibility for family housing and shipment of household goods (applies to active duty, active Reserve, and Reserve Marines serving on EAD as lance corporals and below only).

(6) A statement that the servicewoman will advise the command of any unexpected changes in her medical status and will return to full duty as soon as medically authorized.

(7) A statement that the servicewoman understands that, as soon as medically authorized by an HCP, she will commence physical training in preparation to pass the Marine Corps PFT and conform to acceptable weight standards per reference (b) no later than 6 months following her return to full duty.

c. HCP Notification of Pregnancy to Commanding Officer. Upon confirmation of pregnancy by an HCP, written notification (enclosure (2)) of the servicewoman's condition will be directed to the servicewoman's CO. The HCP notification letter is to be submitted as an enclosure to the servicewoman's notification letter to the CO. The notification letter will include the estimated date of delivery and a determination as to whether any medical reasons exist that make remaining in a full duty status or in the Marine Corps Reserve inadvisable. For purposes of this Order, medical certification of pregnancy by a civilian physician is acceptable.

6. <u>Reporting Requirements</u>

    a. A servicewoman whose pregnancy is confirmed will be reported into the Marine Corps Total Force System (MCTFS) per reference (h). Duty limitations for a pregnant Marine will be reported as DU LIMIT PREGNANCY (limitation code "N") for the period of pregnancy, DU LIMIT MEDICALLY NONDEPLOYABLE (limitation code "D") for the convalescent period following pregnancy and 157 015 DU LIMIT ADMINISTRATIVELY NONDEPLOYABLE (limitation code "TTC") for the deferred deployment period. The HCP Pregnancy Notification letter will be the source document for all diary entries related to pregnancy.

    b. A servicewoman joined to a Status of Resources and Training (SORTS) reporting unit and whose pregnancy is confirmed will be reported into SORTS as non-deployable per reference (i). She will continue to perform normal duties until an HCP certifies that doing so is medically inadvisable.

7. <u>Assignments</u>

    a. The servicewoman shall not be assigned to duties that may adversely affect her health or the health of her unborn child. In consultation with the appropriate HCP, the CO shall determine work assignment limitations. Results of the industrial hygiene site survey, evaluation by the occupational health care provider, or recommendations by the obstetrical health care provider may indicate the need for reassignment or work restriction(s) per reference (j).

    b. A servicewoman reassigned due to pregnancy will be returned to the same billet, in the same command whenever possible, or to an equivalent billet in a command of the same type following the pregnancy, related convalescent leave (42 days), or period of deferment. Permanent change of station (PCS) or temporary additional duty (TAD) orders for school or special duty (i.e., recruiting, drill instructor, etc.) cancelled due to pregnancy will be reissued following the pregnancy and convalescent leave period. A servicewoman who remains qualified is eligible for assignment as long as the assignment/requirement still exists and a school seat is available. Competitive selection boards will reconsider the servicewoman during the next scheduled session. The servicewoman must resubmit the application per applicable directives, as required.

8. <u>Assignment/Deployment Limitations of Pregnant Marines</u>

    a. A pregnant Marine is non-deployable. A servicewoman assigned to a deployed Marine unit who is confirmed pregnant during deployment aboard ship will, at first opportunity, be sent to the closest U.S. military facility that can provide obstetrics/gynecology (OB/GYN) care. The servicewoman will be returned to her unit's home base at the earliest opportunity via a medically authorized mode of transportation.

    b. Pregnant servicewomen may train with their unit, in conjunction with advice from their HCP, up to 20 weeks of pregnancy, when the mode of transportation does not involve transport aboard naval vessels and the deployment is not a contingency operation.

    c. Per reference (k), a servicewoman on an unaccompanied overseas tour who is subsequently confirmed pregnant during her tour, will be reassigned if there are inadequate civilian/military medical facilities with obstetrical capabilities and family housing. The new assignment may be to another overseas location in order to receive credit for an overseas tour. A servicewoman has no actual entitlement to family housing until she has an eligible family member and only then if the CMC (MM) converts the servicewoman's unaccompanied tour to an accompanied tour.

>CH 1 d. Servicewomen will not normally be transferred to deploying units from the time of pregnancy confirmation up to 6 months after the date of delivery. Pregnant Marines are afforded a 6 month deferment from deployment after the date of delivery. The deferment option is provided to the Marine, not the commander. The Marine may waive the deployment deferment period. Commanders have the option of extending this deferment if, in consultation with the HCP, it is deemed necessary for the health of the mother or child.

>CH 1 e. A pregnant servicewoman will not be ordered to a family members restricted tour. Marines will not be assigned to a family members restricted tour for a period of 6 months after the date of delivery. This same opportunity will be afforded a single parent, or the female parent of a dual service couple in the case of adoption. The Marine may waive the deferment period. Commanders have the option of extending this deferment if, in consultation with the HCP, it is deemed necessary for the health of the mother or child.

f. Pregnant servicewomen will be deferred from overseas duty if they are in an advanced stage of pregnancy (greater than 28 weeks) per reference (l).

g. Pregnant servicewomen stationed in CONUS and Hawaii will not be detached after 36 weeks of pregnancy per reference (l). Specific instructions relating to PCS orders modifications or cancellations will be obtained from CMC (Enlisted Assignments Branch (MMEA)/Officer Assignments Branch (MMOA)/Reserve Affairs Division (RA), as appropriate).

h. Pregnant servicewomen serving overseas may be detached at their normal rotation tour date (RTD), provided they do not have to fly after the 28th week of pregnancy per reference (l). Where apparent that the overseas tour of a pregnant Marine will be involuntarily extended because of her condition (e.g., delivery date approximates RTD), CMC (MMEA/MMOA/RA, as appropriate) may authorize early termination of her tour. Normally, CMC (MMEA/MMOA/RA) will not approve early termination of an overseas-restricted tour because of pregnancy where the servicewoman has completed less than 9 months of her tour unless directed by a HCP.

i. Shipboard/Aviation Assignment

(1) Shipboard. Pregnant servicewomen may not embark upon naval vessels, even when the naval vessel is tied to a pier, after the 20th week of pregnancy. Prior to her 20th week of pregnancy, a pregnant servicewoman who is assigned to a ship as part of ship's company may remain onboard ship if the time for medical evacuation of the member to a treatment facility capable of stabilizing obstetric emergencies is less than 6 hours. The 6-hour rule is not intended to allow pregnant women to operate routinely at sea, but rather to provide the CO flexibility during short underway periods such as changes in ship's berth, ammo anchorages, and transits to and from local shipyards.

(2) Aviation

(a) Reference (m) discusses the considerations and requirements regarding pregnant flight personnel. It is imperative that pregnant flight personnel consult with their flight surgeon when they first suspect they are pregnant so that appropriate action can be taken to ensure they receive the necessary prenatal care, and to ensure close monitoring as it relates to the safe conduct of flight.

(b) Pregnancy is considered disqualifying for designated flight personnel unless a medical clearance (waiver) to continue on flight status is granted by CMC (ASM). Waivers may be requested and considered for uncomplicated pregnancies and are valid only until the start of the third trimester (28th week). After the start of the third trimester, all flight personnel are grounded for the remainder of the pregnancy (except for air traffic controllers, as discussed below). Flying during pregnancy is prohibited in single-piloted aircraft, ejection seat aircraft, high-performance aircraft that will operate in excess of 2gs, aircraft involved in shipboard operations, or flights in aircraft with cabin altitudes that will exceed 10,000 feet. This essentially limits waivers to flight personnel who will be flying in transport, maritime, or helo type aircraft with a cabin altitude of less than 10,000 feet. In addition, if an aircrew member becomes pregnant during aviation training, she will be grounded until after completion of the pregnancy. Since participation in aviation physiology and aviation water survival is not permitted during pregnancy, any aircrew member whose qualifications expire during the pregnancy will not be cleared to fly beyond the date of expiration of those qualifications. Aircrew members who have a complicated pregnancy will be considered for waivers on a case-by-case basis.

(c) A request for flight waiver shall be originated by the pregnant servicewoman and submitted per the procedures defined in reference (m) to CMC (ASM) via Naval Operational Medicine Institute Det, Naval Aerospace Medical Institute (NAVOPMEDINST DET NAVAEROMEDINST (Code 342)), 220 Hovey Road, Pensacola, Florida 32508-1044.

(d) As part of the waiver review process, a local board of flight surgeons may issue a temporary Aeromedical Clearance Notice (BUMED 6410/2) to flight personnel following their evaluation and recommendation to CMC for a waiver. This clearance notice is valid until the waiver request is granted or denied by CMC (ASM). However, even though a waiver is granted, changes in the clinical status of the pregnant aircrew member or ergonomic factors that impact her ability to perform safely in the confines of her aircraft may require a flight surgeon to alter the decision and ground the aircrew member in the best interests of the individual and the Marine Corps.

(e) Following the aircrew member's delivery, recovery, and return to full duty status by her obstetrician, a flight surgeon shall submit a post-grounding physical exam to the Naval Aerospace Medical Institute in order to clear the aircrew member for return to full-flight status.

(f) Air Traffic Controllers. An uncomplicated pregnancy of an air traffic controller is not considered physically disqualifying. Duty modifications during pregnancy are expected and should be managed locally to accommodate local circumstances and the individual Marine's medical requirements.

9. General Limitations

a. After confirmation of pregnancy, a pregnant servicewoman shall be exempt from:

>CH 2   (1) Routine physical training and the PFT during pregnancy and for 6 months following return to full duty. However, the servicewoman will participate in an exercise program approved by her OB healthcare provider. A

servicewoman whose pregnancy terminates prematurely or results in a stillborn should inform her command as ordered in paragraph 5b(6) of this order and consult with her OB healthcare provider to determine when it would be advisable to resume physical training and take the PFT.

(2) Exposure to chemical or toxic agents/environmental hazards that are determined unsafe by the cognizant occupational health professional or the health care provider.

(3) Standing at parade rest or attention for longer than 15 minutes.

(4) All routine immunizations except as indicated in reference (l).

(5) Participation in weapons training, swimming qualifications, drown-proofing, and any other physical training requirements that may affect the health of the servicewoman/fetus. Diving duty is hazardous and carries an increased hyperbaric risk to the fetus; therefore, any type of diving during pregnancy is prohibited.

b. The pregnant servicewoman may be allowed to work shifts.

10. Specific Limitations. During the last 3 months of pregnancy (weeks 28 and beyond) the servicewoman shall be:

a. Allowed to rest 20 minutes every 4 hours (sitting in a chair with feet up is acceptable).

b. Limited to a 40-hour workweek. The 40 hours may be distributed among any 7-day period, but hours are defined by the servicewoman's presence at her duty station, and not by type of work performed. Pregnancy does not remove a servicewoman from watch standing responsibilities, but all hours shall count as part of the 40 hour per week limitation. In instances where the unit work week/watch standing requirements exceed 40 hours, the CO, in consultation with the HCP, must be informed and approve, on a case-by-case basis, extension of the servicewoman's work week beyond 40 hours. The servicewoman may request a work waiver to extend her hours beyond the stated 40-hour week, if she is physically capable and her OB HCP concurs.

11. Medical Considerations for Work Assignments

a. General. Few restrictions are required in an uncomplicated pregnancy of a physically fit, trained servicewoman working in a safe environment.

b. Work Reassignment. The servicewoman shall not be assigned to duties where she may be exposed to a reproductive/developmental hazard to herself, or other, including her developing fetus. A pregnant servicewoman's duties/occupation may cause or exacerbate symptoms such as lightheadedness or nausea. In consultation with the appropriate HCP, the CO shall determine work assignment limitations. The results of the industrial hygiene site survey, evaluation by the occupational HCP, or recommendations of the OB HCP may indicate the need for reassignment or work restriction(s) per reference (j). Common restrictions from duty fall into the following categories:

(1) <u>Medical</u>. Clinical conditions as identified by the servicewoman's OB HCP.

(2) <u>Environmental</u>. The work environment may expose a pregnant servicewoman to potential health hazards. The occupational HCP will determine appropriate restrictions as detailed in reference (j).

(3) <u>Ergonomic</u>. Instances where there may be no obvious medical contraindications, but where the individual's physical configuration/abilities prohibit participation (such as lying in a prone position for weapons qualifications, certain duty aboard ships, etc.) or where nausea or fatigability would be hazardous to the servicewoman, the unborn child, or other servicemembers of the unit.

(4) <u>Other</u>. Areas of questionably harmful effects such as chemical, biological, radiological and nuclear effects (CBRNE) training, a regular unit physical training program and certain unit qualification tests or hands on elements of skills qualification tests.

12. <u>Inoculations</u>

a. It has been determined that live virus immunizations can be hazardous to an unborn child if conception occurs within 3 months of vaccination.

b. Medical personnel will ask servicewomen if they are pregnant (lab testing is NOT required). If the answer is YES, the immunization is to be deferred. If the answer is MAYBE, refer the servicewoman for evaluation. If the answer is NO, immunize the servicewoman.

c. If live virus vaccine is administered, servicewomen are to be counseled to avoid becoming pregnant for 3 months. This counseling will be documented in the servicewoman's health record.

13. <u>OB/GYN Care - General</u>

a. Per reference (a), servicewomen assigned to imminently deploying units or positions (defined as scheduled to deploy within 3 months) will be given priority over other active duty personnel receiving routine OB/GYN care in all medical facilities.

b. Active duty servicewomen may obtain OB/GYN care at civilian hospitals in limited circumstances per reference (g). This is not a routine option, and servicewomen should be familiar with the specific procedures for seeking civilian care to avoid significant financial liability for which there is no reimbursement. References (l) and (n) provide detailed information regarding civilian maternity care.

14. <u>Convalescent Leave</u>

a. The servicewoman's CO may grant a period of convalescent leave for an active duty servicewoman who is not fit for duty and requires additional medical care as recommended by her OB HCP. The length of convalescent leave will normally be 42 days after discharge from the MTF following any uncomplicated vaginal delivery or cesarean section. The servicewoman may terminate leave earlier with approval from an HCP.

b. It is the responsibility of the servicewoman to report any complications or medical problems that she has experienced during convalescent leave to her attending physician. The attending physician may then recommend an extension beyond the standard 42 days based on the servicewoman's clinical circumstances. The HCP must certify that the patient is not fit for duty, will not need hospitalization during the contemplated convalescent leave period, and that such leave will not delay the final disposition of the patient. The servicewoman's permanent command must be notified of this recommendation.

15. Support of Servicewomen With Nursing Infants

    a. Servicewomen who desire to continue breastfeeding upon return to duty will notify their chain of command at the earliest possible time to allow the command to determine how best to support them and facilitate the prompt evaluation of the workplace for potential hazards.

    b. When possible, the servicewoman who continues to provide breast milk to her infant upon return to duty shall be, at a minimum, afforded the availability of a clean, secluded space (not a toilet space) with ready access to a water source for the purpose of pumping breast milk.

    c. The time required for breast milk expression varies and is highly dependent upon several factors including the age of the infant, amount of milk produced, pump quality, the distance the pumping location is from the workplace, as well as how conveniently located the water source is from the pump location. Supervisors and lactating servicewomen will collaborate to keep to a minimum the amount of time required for milk expression. Lactation consultants are available at the MTF to assist in this endeavor.

16. Adoption

    a. Infants Placed for Adoption. Pregnant servicewomen intending to place their infant for adoption are not eligible for OCONUS assignment until delivery and adoption requirements are completed. Initial guidance and assistance for placing infants for adoption can be obtained from the local Marine Corps Legal Assistance Office (MCLAO). Servicewomen intending to place their infants for adoption will meet with the appropriate legal counsel and placement agencies to ensure specific state requirements are followed.

    b. Marines Adopting an Infant/Child. The CO may authorize up to 10 days permissive TAD for any Marine adopting a child, dependent on the unit's mission, specific operational circumstances, and the Marine's billet. This authorization extends to both members in a dual military status. The permissive TAD period should commence when the child is ready for placement in order to assist the parent(s) in relocating the adopted child, formalizing legal requirements, establishing a child care program, and other tasks as required.

17. Extension of Active Duty/Reenlistment

    a. Enlisted Marines, including AR Marines, who are pregnant may reenlist/extend, provided they are otherwise qualified per reference (o).

    b. Per reference (p), pregnant Reserve officers may apply for extensions of up to 1 year on their current period of obligated service.

18. Separation from Active Duty

    a. Upon medical certification of pregnancy, a Marine may request separation by submitting an Administrative Action Form (NAVMC 10274) to the appropriate separation authority as defined by reference (q). References (c) and (q) provide for separations for the convenience of the Government by reason of parenthood or by reason of dependency or hardship should a servicewoman become unable to fulfill military obligations or become unavailable for worldwide assignment.

    b. A pregnant servicewoman may voluntarily request separation; however, the request will normally be denied unless there are extenuating circumstances (which the servicewoman can substantiate by demonstrating overriding or compelling factors of personal need) or there are extraordinary circumstances of a humanitarian nature that exist. Reference (q) pertains.

    c. A servicewoman may not be involuntarily separated on the basis of pregnancy. However, pregnancy does not bar processing for separation for other reasons under the appropriate paragraph of reference (q). For example, a pregnant servicewoman who is being processed for separation based on misconduct or commission of a serious offense may still be separated on the latter basis. The care and management of pregnant servicewomen prisoners confined to a brig shall conform to the requirements of this Order, with the exception that convalescent leave cannot be authorized. Pregnancy, per se, does not preclude confinement in a brig as long as appropriate prenatal care is provided and there is a MTF near the brig that can provide for labor, delivery, and the management of OB emergencies.

    d. During the separation physical examination process, if the HCP determines that a servicewoman is pregnant, no additional examination; i.e., obstetrical exam, is required. Pregnancy does not disqualify a servicewoman from separating from the military. The servicewoman should be informed concerning maternity benefits available to her after separation.

    e. The servicewoman (active, AR, and reservists on EAD) will provide a statement of understanding acknowledging eligibility for maternity care following her release from active duty/discharge. Additionally, per reference (g), a former servicewoman loses her entitlement to civilian maternity care regardless of the circumstances. Refer to paragraph 20 of this Order for details concerning maternity care after separation from active duty.

    f. Separation for pregnancy must be effected no later than 4 weeks prior to the estimated date of delivery; however, an earlier separation date may be requested. All such requests must include specific justification for separation, per reference (q).

    g. An officer's request for resignation/release from active duty will comply with references (l), (r), and (q).

    h. COs will forward the servicewoman's request for separation to the separation authority with a recommendation for separation or retention on active duty.

    i. To prevent the loss of potential mobilization assets, the separation authority will screen servicewomen being separated for pregnancy for transfer to the IRR vice discharge per reference (q).

19. Reserve Marines

    a. A pregnant Reserve Marine serving in the SMCR without a service obligation may transfer to the IRR at her own request. A pregnant Reserve Marine with a mandatory service obligation must submit a request to transfer to the IRR, via the appropriate chain of command, to the Commander, Marine Forces Reserve or Commanding General, MOBCOM (for IMA personnel), as applicable. An SMCR Marine (either obligor or nonobligor) and a member of the IRR who desire a discharge must submit a written request to the Commander, Marine Forces Reserve or Commanding General, MOBCOM (for IMA personnel), as appropriate.

>CH 1 b. A pregnant Reserve Marine will not be allowed to perform any periods of Inactive Duty for Training (IDT) within 30-days of her anticipated date of delivery, nor will a pregnant Reserve Marine be issued active duty orders (with or without pay) after 28-weeks of pregnancy. Unit commanders will not require Marines to perform IDT periods within 30-days of the anticipated delivery date or annual training (AT) after 28-weeks of pregnancy. Alternate at and rescheduled IDTS may be authorized. Prior to the issuance of orders, medical documentation should be provided that will verify the estimated date of delivery and that there are no complications that have arisen since the onset of the pregnancy.

>CH 1 c. After giving birth, a Reserve servicewoman will not be required to perform active duty for 4 months (applies to those Marines not on EAD) or active duty orders or IDT for 6 weeks after giving birth.

    (1) This policy is also applicable to single female parents and one parent of a dual service couple in the case of adoption. In the case of adoption, the 4-month/6-week period (as applicable) starts after the actual effective date of the adoption of a child.

    (2) The reservist may waive any part of the deferment period. If the deferment is not waived and the unit performs AT, the reservist will attend an alternate AT.

20. Maternity Care After Separation

    a. Under the law, neither the military departments nor TRICARE have the authority to pay civilian maternity care expenses for former servicewomen who separate from active duty while they are pregnant, regardless of the circumstances requiring the use of civilian facilities. A former servicewoman loses her entitlement to all civilian maternity care at military expense upon the effective date of separation as shown on DD Form 214 (DD Form 214). Prior to separation, a servicewoman should be encouraged to consult with a health benefits advisor for current information regarding health benefits available to former active duty personnel.

    b. Active duty and Reserve members who are pregnant upon separating from active duty under honorable conditions with a DD Form 214 have several options available for maternity benefits. The options are as follows:

    (1) Pregnant servicewomen who are separating from active duty may purchase temporary civilian health insurance through the Continued Health Care Benefit Program (CHCBP). CHCBP is a DoD-sponsored health insurance program that is available to honorably discharged service members and can provide coverage for 18 to 36 months following separation. CHCBP provides

health care coverage for pre-existing conditions, which include pregnancy. The service member must enroll in the program within 60 days following discharge from active military service. Additional information on CHCBP is available at www.humana-military.com.

(2) The service secretaries (under special administrative authority) allow former servicewomen, who are pregnant and separate under honorable conditions, to receive maternity care through the Ex-Service Maternity Care Benefit. This benefit provides for prenatal care, delivery, and up to 6 weeks of postnatal care at an MTF per reference (g). The decision to grant the servicewoman this benefit is determined by the MTF CO and is based on the capability of the MTF to provide maternity care on a space available basis. Servicewomen must present their DD Form 214 to the Health Administration Office of the MTF when applying for maternity care. The following criteria should be considered when making the decision:

(a) The servicewoman presents documented evidence that reflects that a physical examination given at an MTF demonstrates that she was pregnant prior to her separation from active duty.

(b) The MTF to which she applies for care has the capability of providing maternity care. Many MTFs cannot provide maternity care. A pregnant servicewoman who elects to leave the service must first consider the distance between her home and the nearest MTF that does have maternity care capability. She must consider the possibilities of premature delivery or other emergency maternity care needs. These factors could unexpectedly force her to use a civilian source of care. Should that happen, neither the military departments, TRICARE, nor the Veterans Administration (VA) has authority to pay civilian maternity care expenses, regardless of the circumstances necessitating use of civilian care for either the ex-servicewoman or her newborn infant. The servicewoman should be aware that if the newborn infant requires care beyond that which is available at the MTF, it may be necessary to transfer the infant to a civilian source of care (e.g., neonatal care) and these expenses will be the servicewoman's personal financial responsibility. However, every effort will be made to send the infant to an MTF.

(c) Before deciding to accept a discharge or resign from the service, a pregnant servicewoman should contact the Health Benefits Advisor of the MTF that she plans to use, to determine if the:

1 facility provides maternity care,

2 facility is close enough to her planned place of residence to provide her assurance that, barring emergency requirements, she can reach it expeditiously at the time of birth, and

3 facility's workload will permit acceptance of her case.

(3) Pregnant active duty and Reserve servicewomen separating from active duty under honorable conditions with a DD Form 214 or who possess a DD Form 214 from prior military service are eligible for maternity care through the VA health system. VA facilities are using enhanced sharing authority to contract for obstetrical services to include prenatal care, childbirth, and post-partum care. In some cases, some of the expenses incurred may be the

responsibility of the servicewoman. This benefit does not, at this time,
cover care of the newborn. Prior to separation, servicewomen should contact
the women veterans' coordinator for the area in which they will be residing
to expedite the administrative process for eligibility. The women veterans
coordinators directory, eligibility requirements, and other benefits can be
located on the following website; http://www.va.gov/womenvet/.

(4) Pregnant active duty and Reserve servicewomen (who are separating
from active duty after being called up or ordered in support of a contingency
operation for an active duty period of more than 30 days) may be eligible for
the Transition Assistance Management Program (TAMP). This Program offers
transitional TRICARE coverage for eligible beneficiaries. The servicewomen
should consult with a health benefits advisor for current information
regarding this health care benefit.

21. Action

a. Commanding officers will:

(1) Maintain a command environment that promotes the education of
male and female Marines concerning the enduring individual responsibilities
of family planning and parenthood.

(2) Thoroughly counsel each pregnant servicewoman (and their partner
in the case where both are in the same command) on the contents of this
Order.

(3) Ensure that deploying servicewomen assigned to their unit/
command report to the medical department for pregnancy testing NET 14 and NLT
10 days prior to deployment in order to prevent the deployment of a pregnant
Marine.

(4) Ensure that a pregnant servicewoman who has the potential for
exposure to occupational reproductive/developmental hazards in the workplace
is afforded the opportunity for counseling by an occupational health care
provider per reference (j). The occupational exposures of Reproductive or
Developmental Concern questionnaires (enclosures (3) and (4)) shall be
completed by the pregnant servicewoman and command supervisory personnel
knowledgeable of the servicewoman's workplace. If potential for exposure to
a developmental hazard is present in the workplace, or if naval activities
have not determined the possibility of such potential, the command shall
arrange for an occupational health care provider to evaluate the servicewoman
as soon as possible. If the most recent industrial hygiene site survey
documents that no potential for exposure to a developmental hazard exists in
the workplace, then an occupational medicine evaluation should occur if
either the pregnant servicewoman or the CO requests it. A copy of the
appropriate sections of the completed evaluations should be placed in the
servicewoman's medical record and in the servicewoman's command safety office
file.

(5) Ensure that a pregnant Marine is not required to perform duties,
including physical training that, in the opinion of the HCP, are hazardous to
her or the unborn child.

(6) Ensure that a servicewoman who will become a single parent and
Marines who are members of a dual military couple residing in a joint
household are counseled regarding the availability of government housing
(especially in high cost areas).

(7) Ensure that pregnant servicewomen may deploy in conjunction with advice from the HCP, per paragraph 8 of this Order. These determinations will be made on a case-by-case basis and will be dependent on the unit's mission, the servicewoman's billet, available medical support, and medical authorization.

(8) Ensure that a servicewoman returns to a normal duty assignment commensurate with her grade, MOS, and the unit's requirements when the HCP certifies that the servicewoman is medically qualified for full duty. This will normally occur after the 42 days convalescent leave period following an uncomplicated delivery. A servicewoman needing additional personal time, after being medically certified fit for duty, may be granted annual leave per reference (s).

(9) Ensure that pregnant servicewomen are not adversely evaluated or receive adverse fitness reports or evaluations as a consequence of pregnancy. Pregnancy shall not be mentioned in the comments section. Weight standards exceeded during pregnancy are not cause for adverse fitness reports or evaluations. Pregnant servicewomen who have recently delivered, who are otherwise fully qualified for and desire reenlistment, but who exceed acceptable weight standards per reference (b) will be extended for the maximum of up to 6 months after delivery.

(10) Ensure that a servicewoman whose pregnancy terminates prematurely, or results in a stillbirth, provides documentation from a HCP that she is fit for full duty. A command climate of concerned leadership is essential in helping the servicewoman impacted by these types of traumatic events.

(11) Ensure that male and female Marines are afforded the opportunity to take advantage of available legal assistance for advice regarding their options in establishing paternity. Absent a court order or other competent authority, the servicemember will not be compelled to have a paternity test. Department of the Navy medical facilities do not pay for paternity testing. Paternity testing will be obtained at the servicemember's expense.

b. Commanding officers may:

(1) Authorize (per servicewoman's request) a pregnant servicewoman to occupy off-base housing and be paid BAH up to her 20th week of pregnancy, per reference (a). From the 20th week onward the host commander must approve a request to occupy off-base housing. (See paragraph 4d of this Order.)

(2) Authorize a pregnant servicewoman to wear either the maternity or camouflage work uniform when it is determined that the standard uniforms can no longer be worn. The servicewoman is expected to wear regular uniforms upon returning from convalescent leave; however, COs may approve the wearing of maternity uniforms up to 6 months from the date of delivery based on an HCP's diagnosis and/or recommendations. Reference (t) prescribes regulations regarding the wearing of the maternity uniform. Reference (u) prescribes regulations regarding the procurement of the maternity uniform. The CO may authorize a servicewoman to wear the utility uniform in lieu of the maternity uniform during early pregnancy and after return to duty when the uniform of the day is normally Service "C", "B", or Blue Dress "D".

c. <u>HCP</u>

(1) The HCP is responsible for ensuring the privacy of the servicewoman while at the same time safeguarding both her welfare and that of the unborn child.

(2) When pregnancy is confirmed, there are related matters not strictly medical, about which the HCP is called upon to aid in rendering a decision. Each HCP, with the responsibility for pregnancy confirmation and/or prenatal care, should be familiar with the administrative and command requirements related to pregnant servicewomen.

(3) The HCP is responsible for reviewing, in its entirety, reference (l) which provides detailed information concerning the administrative and medical management of pregnant servicewomen and includes the following:

        (a) HCP responsibilities

        (b) Immunizations

        (c) Light duty

        (d) Problem pregnancy

        (e) Medical holding company

        (f) Admission to MTF

        (g) LIMDU boards

        (h) Quarters-OB status

        (i) Hospitalization

        (j) Postnatal care

        (k) Termination of pregnancy

d. <u>DC, Manpower & Reserve Affairs (M&RA)</u>

(1) Manpower Management Information Systems Division (MI) will assist in extracting information from the Operational Data Store enterprise (ODSE) on the number of discharges for pregnancy by fiscal year (FY). This will assist the Manpower Integration & Analysis Section (MPP-50), in studying the issues surrounding pregnancy and Director, Manpower Plans & Policy Division (MP) in meeting the reporting requirements per reference (a).

(2) MP Division has cognizance on the policy contained in this Order. They will coordinate the effort to meet the reporting requirements to Assistant Secretary of the Navy (M&RA) per reference (a).

e. <u>DC, Aviation (AVN)</u>. Will ensure that procedures for managing requests for flight waivers are disseminated throughout the aviation community and remain in accordance with reference (l).

f. Director, Health Services (HS). Will collaborate with BUMED in the development, maintenance, change, and promulgation of policy regarding the medical management and medically related administrative issues concerning pregnant servicewomen.

g. Chaplain of the Marine Corps (RFL). Will ensure that COs and Marines are supported by chaplains fully prepared to provide counsel and advice concerning issues of faith and character, parental responsibilities, personal decisions, and core values per reference (a).

h. Staff Judge Advocate to CMC (SJA). Will coordinate to ensure that appropriate judge advocates provide legal assistance relating to Marines' options in establishing paternity and obtaining child support.

i. CG MCCDC. Will ensure classes in sexually responsible behavior are:

(1) Presented during entry-level training to both officer and enlisted Marines.

(2) Incorporated as part of the leadership training presented in all PME courses.

(3) Additionally, the CG MCCDC will ensure the policy contained in this Order and classes on sexually responsible behavior are incorporated into the annual training requirements contained in the Marine Corps Common Skills Program.

(4) Additionally, TECOM will ensure Marines are properly educated at entry-level training, Professional Military Education (PME) courses, and annually in Troop Information Programs on the following subjects:

(a) Core Values.

(b) Expectations regarding responsible behavior.

(c) The broad range of services available to assist and encourage our Marines in making decisions that are supportive of both service obligations and parental responsibilities.

22. Reserve Applicability. This Order is applicable to the Marine Corps Total Force.

W. L. NYLAND
Assistant Commandant
of the Marine Corps

DISTRIBUTION: PCN 10207020800

    Copy to: 7000110 (55)
               7000260 (2)
               7000144/8145001 (1)

PREGNANCY AND PARENTING POLICY TASKS AND RESPONSIBILITIES

Date Signed: 3/18/2005
MARADMIN Number: 133/05

R 181500Z MAR 05
FM CMC WASHINGTON DC(UC)
TO AL MARADMIN(UC)
UNCLASSIFIED//
MARADMIN 133/05
MSGID/GENADMIN/CMC WASHINGTON DC//
SUBJ/PREGNANCY AND PARENTING POLICY TASKS AND RESPONSIBILITIES//
REF/A/DOC/MCO 5000.12E/-//
NARR/REF A MCO 5000.12E, MARINE CORPS POLICY CONCERNING PREGNANCY
AND PARENTHOOD.//
POC/MSGID/GENADMIN/CMC WASHINGTON DC MRA/MPO40/-//
GENTEXT/REMARKS/1. PURPOSE. THIS MESSAGE CLARIFIES AND HELPS
FACILITATE THE PROMULGATION OF THE POLICY AND GUIDANCE CONCERNING
PREGNANCY AND PARENTHOOD AS SET FORTH IN THE REFERENCE.
2. MCO 5000.12E, THE MARINE CORPS'PREGNANCY AND PARENTHOOD POLICY,
WAS SIGNED ON 8 DECEMBER 2004 AND HAS BEEN ACCESSIBLE SINCE
1 FEBRUARY 2005. THIS MARADMIN REITERATES TO COMMANDERS AND UNIT
PERSONNEL THEIR INDIVIDUAL AND UNIT RESPONSIBILITIES TO ENSURE
THE SAFETY OF PREGNANT MARINES.
3. TASKS AND RESPONSIBILITIES UNDER THE NEW POLICY:
A. PRIOR TO RECEIVING LIVE VIRUS INOCULATIONS, FEMALE MARINES WILL
BE COUNSELED CONCERNING THEIR LIKELIHOOD OF BEING PREGNANT AND
THE RISKS ASSOCIATED WITH RECEIVING THESE INOCULATIONS.
(1) IT HAS BEEN DETERMINED THAT LIVE VIRUS IMMUNIZATIONS CAN BE
HAZARDOUS TO THE FETUS OR AN UNBORN CHILD.
(2) IF LIVE VIRUS VACCINE IS ADMINISTERED, SERVICEWOMEN WILL BE
COUNSELED TO AVOID BECOMING PREGNANT FOR 3 MONTHS FOLLOWING
INOCULATION.
B. COMMANDING OFFICERS WILL ENSURE THAT ALL FEMALE MARINES IN THEIR
UNIT ARE ADMINISTERED A PREGNANCY TEST 10-14 DAYS PRIOR TO DEPLOYING.
URINALYSIS OR BLOOD TESTING IS THE ONLY PREGNANCY SCREENING
AUTHORIZED.
C. COMMANDING OFFICERS WILL ENSURE THAT THE PROPER ADMINISTRATIVE
ACTIONS ARE COMPLETED FOR PREGNANT MARINES.
(1) THE LETTER FROM THE MARINE, WITH HEALTH CARE PROVIDER'S LETTER
ENCLOSED, INFORMING COMMANDING OFFICER OF PREGNANCY CONFIRMATION IS
THE SOURCE DOCUMENT FOR ALL DEFERMENTS ASSOCIATED WITH THE PREGNANCY.
(2) THE PROPER DUTY LIMIT CODE "N" MUST BE REPORTED WITHIN THE
MARINE CORPS TOTAL FORCE SYSTEM VIA A UNIT DIARY ENTRY.
D. PREGNANT MARINES ARE NON-DEPLOYABLE. COMMANDING OFFICERS WILL
ENSURE THAT THEY DO NOT DEPLOY. THIS IS NOT A PERSONAL OR UNIT
DRIVEN CHOICE AND ALL PERSONNEL CONCERNED MUST COMPLY WITH THIS
POLICY.
E. PREGNANT MARINES ARE AFFORDED A 12-MONTH DEPLOYMENT/RESTRICTED
TOUR DEFERMENT OPTION FROM THE DATE OF DELIVERY. THE ORDER PROVIDES
THE OPTION TO THE MARINE, NOT THE COMMANDER. THE MARINE SHOULD NOT
BE PRESSURED EITHER WAY TO DECIDE WHETHER OR NOT TO WAIVE THE
DEFERMENT.
4. COMMANDERS CAN DOWNLOAD MCO 5000.12E AT WWW.USMC.MIL. HQMC POC/
T.J. OWENS/CAPT/COML 703-784-9387/DSN 278-9387//

MARADMIN 027/07

«« --- »»

Date signed: 01/19/2007   **MARADMIN Number:**   027/07

Subject: CHANGE 1 TO MARINE CORPS POLICY CONCERNING PREGNANCY AND PARENTHOOD

191516Z JAN 07
CMC WASHINGTON DC(UC)
AL MARADMIN(UC)
MARADMIN
MARADMIN 027/07
MSGID/GENADMIN/CMC WASHINGTON DC MRA MP//
SUBJ/CHANGE 1 TO MARINE CORPS POLICY CONCERNING PREGNANCY
/AND PARENTHOOD//
REF/A/MSGID:DOC/MCO 5000.12E/-//
POC/S. T. FOSTER/CAPT/MPO/-/TEL:703-784-9387
/TEL:DSN 278-9387//
NARR/REF A MCO 5000.12E, MARINE CORPS POLICY CONCERNING
PREGNANCY AND PARENTHOOD.//
GENTEXT/REMARKS/1. PURPOSE. THIS MESSAGE MAKES CHANGES TO
MCO 5000.12E REGARDING THE RELEASE FROM ACTIVE DUTY OF
PREGNANT RESERVE MARINES.
2. EFFECTIVE IMMEDIATELY, RESERVE MARINES ON ACTIVE DUTY
ORDERS WILL NO LONGER BE SEPARATED FROM ACTIVE DUTY DUE TO
PREGNANCY. PARAGRAPH 19.B OF MCO 5000.12E IS CANCELLED
AND REPLACED WITH THE FOLLOWING PARAGRAPH, "A PREGNANT RESERVE
MARINE WILL NOT BE ALLOWED TO PERFORM ANY PERIODS
OF INACTIVE DUTY FOR TRAINING (IDT) WITHIN 30-DAYS OF HER
ANTICIPATED DATE OF DELIVERY, NOR WILL A PREGNANT RESERVE
MARINE BE ISSUED ACTIVE DUTY ORDERS (WITH OR WITHOUT PAY)
AFTER 28-WEEKS OF PREGNANCY. UNIT COMMANDERS WILL NOT
REQUIRE MARINES TO PERFORM IDT PERIODS WITHIN 30-DAYS OF
THE ANTICIPATED DELIVERY DATE OR ANNUAL TRAINING (AT)
AFTER 28-WEEKS OF PREGNANCY. ALTERNATE AT AND RESCHEDULED
IDTS MAY BE AUTHORIZED. PRIOR TO THE ISSUANCE OF ORDERS,
MEDICAL DOCUMENTATION SHOULD BE PROVIDED THAT WILL VERIFY
THE ESTIMATED DATE OF DELIVERY AND THAT THERE ARE NO
COMPLICATIONS THAT HAVE ARISEN SINCE THE ONSET OF THE
PREGNANCY."
3. IN PARAGRAPH 19.C AFTER "APPLIES TO THOSE MARINES NOT
ON EAD", ADD THE PHRASE "OR ACTIVE DUTY ORDERS".
4. THE POLICY GOVERNING PREGNANT ACTIVE DUTY MARINES WILL
ALSO GOVERN RESERVE MARINES SERVING ON ACTIVE DUTY.
5. COMMANDERS CAN DOWNLOAD MCO 5000.12E AT WWW.USMC.MIL. //

PCN 10207020801

DISTRIBUTION STATEMENT A: Approved for public release; distribution
is unlimited

MARADMIN 358/07

«« -- »»

Date signed: 06/14/2007   **MARADMIN Number:** 358/07

Subject: CHANGE 2 TO MARINE CORPS POLICY CONCERNING PREGNANCY AND PARENTHOOD

```
UNCLAS 121926Z JUN 07
CMC WASHINGTON DC(UC)
AL MARADMIN(UC)
MARADMIN 358/07
MSGID/GENADMIN/CMC WASHINGTON DC MRA/MP DIV//
SUBJ/CHANGE 2 TO MARINE CORPS POLICY CONCERNING PREGNANCY AND
/PARENTHOOD//
REF/A/MSGID:GENADMIN/CMC WASHINGTON DC/YMD:20050318//
REF/B/MSGID:DOC/MCO 5000.12E/-//
POC/S. T. FOSTER/CAPT/MPO-40/-/TEL:703-784-9387/TEL:DSN 278-9387//
NARR/REF A IS MARADMIN 133/05, PREGNANCY AND PARENTING POLICY
TASKS AND RESPONSIBILITIES. REF B IS MCO 5000.12E, MARINE CORPS
POLICY CONCERING PREGNANCY AND PARENTHOOD.//
GENTEXT/REMARKS/1.  PURPOSE.  THIS MESSAGE CANCELS PARAGRAPH 3.E
OF MARADMIN 133/05 AND MAKES CHANGES TO MCO 5000.12E, MARINE
CORPS POLICY CONCERNING PREGNANCY AND PARENTHOOD.
2.  CHANGE TO MARADMIN 133/05:
A.  EFFECTIVE IMMEDIATELY, PARAGRAPH 3.E, WHICH STATES, "PREGNANT
MARINES ARE AFFORDED A 12-MONTH DEPLOYMENT/RESTRICTED TOUR
DEFERMENT OPTION FROM THE DATE OF DELIVERY.  THE ORDER PROVIDES
THE OPTION TO THE MARINE, NOT THE COMMANDER.  THE MARINE SHOULD
NOT BE PRESSURED EITHER WAY TO DECIDE WHETHER OR NOT TO WAIVE
THE DEFERMENT," IS CANCELLED.
3.  CHANGES TO MCO 5000.12E ARE AS FOLLOWS:
A.  REPLACE PARAGRAPH 8.D WITH THE FOLLOWING PARAGRAPH,
"SERVICEWOMEN WILL NOT NORMALLY BE TRANSFERRED TO DEPLOYING UNITS
FROM THE TIME OF PREGNANCY CONFIRMATION UP TO 6 MONTHS AFTER THE DATE OF
DELIVERY.
PREGNANT MARINES ARE AFFORDED A 6 MONTH DEFERMENT FROM DEPLOYMENT AFTER THE
DATE OF DELIVERY.  THE DEFERMENT OPTION IS PROVIDED TO THE MARINE, NOT THE
COMMANDER.  THE MARINE MAY WAIVE THE DEPLOYMENT DEFERMENT PERIOD.  COMMANDERS
HAVE THE OPTION OF EXTENDING THIS DEFERMENT IF, IN CONSULTATION WITH THE HCP,
IT IS DEEMED NECESSARY FOR THE HEALTH OF THE MOTHER OR CHILD."
B.  REPLACE PARAGRAPH 8.E WITH THE FOLLOWING PARAGRAPH, "A PREGNANT
SERVICEWOMAN WILL NOT BE ORDERED TO A FAMILY MEMBERS RESTRICTED TOUR.
MARINES WILL NOT BE ASSIGNED TO A FAMILY MEMBERS RETRICTED TOUR FOR A PERIOD
OF 6 MONTHS AFTER THE DATE OF DELIVERY.  THIS SAME OPPORTUNITY WILL BE
AFFORDED A SINGLE PARENT, OR THE FEMALE PARENT OF A DUAL SERVICE COUPLE IN
```

PCN 10207020802

DISTRIBUTION STATEMENT A: Approved for public release; distribution is unlimited

THE CASE OF ADOPTION. THE MARINE MAY WAIVE THE DEFERMENT PERIOD. COMMANDERS
HAVE THE OPTION OF EXTENDING THIS DEFERMENT IF, IN CONSULTATION WITH THE HCP,
IT IS DEEMED NECESSARY FOR THE HEALTH OF THE MOTHER OR CHILD."
C. THE FIRST SENTENCE OF PARAGRAPH 9.A(1) IS IN CONTRADICTION WITH PARAGRAPH
4.A(6). PARAGRAPH 9.A(1) IS CANCELLED AND REPLACED WITH THE FOLLOWING,
(AFTER CONFIRMATION OF PREGNANCY, A PREGNANT SERVICEWOMAN SHALL BE EXEMPT
FROM), "ROUTINE PHYSICAL TRAINING AND THE PFT DURING PREGNANCY AND FOR 6
MONTHS FOLLOWING RETURN TO FULL DUTY. HOWEVER, THE SERVICEWOMAN WILL
PARTICIPATE IN AN EXERCISE PROGRAM APPROVED BY HER OB HEALTHCARE PROVIDER. A
SERVICEWOMAN WHOSE PREGNANCY TERMINATES PREMATURELY OR RESULTS IN A STILLBORN
SHOULD INFORM HER COMMAND AS ORDERED IN PARAGRAPH 5B(6) OF THIS ORDER AND
CONSULT WITH HER OB HEALTHCARE PROVDIER TO DETERMINE WHEN IT WOULD BE
ADVISABLE TO RESUME PHYSICAL TRAINING AND TAKE THE PFT."
4. MARINES WHO HAVE DELIVERED AND ARE ON THE TWELVE MONTH DEFERMENT WILL
REMAIN NON-DEPLOYABLE FOR TWELVE MONTHS FROM THEIR DELIVERY DATE. MARINES
WHO HAVE NOT DELIVERED FROM THE AUTHORIZATION DATE OF THIS MARADMIN WILL USE
THE GUIDANCE CONTAINED IN THIS MARADMIN.
5. COMMANDERS CAN DOWNLOAD MCO 5000.12E AT WWW.USMC.MIL.//

FORMAT FOR COMMANDING OFFICER NOTIFICATION

5000.12
Date

From: Servicewoman's Grade, Full Name, SSN/PMOS, USMC(R)
To: Commanding Officer

Subj: FORMAT FOR SERVICEMEMBER NOTIFICATION OF PREGANACY/ADOPTION TO
       COMMANDING OFFICER

Ref: (a) MCO 5000.12E
       (b) MCO 1740.13A
       (c) MCO P1900.16
       (d) BUMEDINST 6320.3B

Encl: (1) Medical Certification of Pregnancy
       (2) Separation Request (only if applicable)

1. I have been fully counseled and understand the contents of reference (a) and provide the following information:

    a. This is to notify the command of my pregnancy. A medical certificate of pregnancy is provided as enclosure (1) and includes the estimated date of delivery and whether any medical reasons exist which make remaining in a full duty status inadvisable.

    b. I understand that I am responsible for making arrangements for child care during regular working hours, duty, exercises, war or combat contingency deployment, etc., and will develop a Family Care Plan per reference (b). (Applies to Active Component, AR, and Reserve Marines serving EAD only.) I understand that I am responsible for making arrangements for child care during periods of active duty/inactive duty for training and upon mobilization. (Applies to SMCR Marines only.)

    c. I understand that I remain otherwise eligible for reenlistment and will serve on active duty until the expiration of my active service obligation. (Applies to Active Component, AR, and Reserve Marines serving EAD only. A SMCR Marine will indicate that she will remain in the SMCR.)

    d. I understand that I may request separation per reference (c) and may remain eligible for maternity care until the birth of my child in limited circumstances per reference (d). Select only one of the following two sentences:

        Option A: If I feel that extenuating circumstances exist which preclude my further service, I understand that I must request for separation per paragraph 18 of reference (a).

        Option B: Since I feel that extenuating circumstances exist which preclude my further service, enclosure (2) is my request for separation per paragraph 18 of reference (a).

ENCLOSURE (1)

1

MCO 5000.12E
08 DEC 04

Subj: FORMAT FOR SERVICEMEMBER NOTIFICATION OF PREGANACY/ADOPTION TO
       COMMANDING OFFICER

    e. I understand that I remain available for worldwide assignment and
that there is no guarantee of special consideration in duty assignments or
duty stations based solely on my pregnancy or the fact that I will have a
dependent, except as provided for in reference (a).

    f. I am aware of the limitations of eligibility for dependent housing
and shipment of household goods (applies to Active Component, AR, and Reserve
Marines serving on EAD as E-4's and below).

2. I will advise the command of any unexpected changes in my medical status
and will return to full duty as soon as medically authorized.

3. I understand that I must be prepared to pass the Marine Corps Physical
Fitness Test and conform to the acceptable weight standards no later than 6
months following my return to full duty. I will commence physical training as
soon as medically authorized.

_____

Service member's Signature

_____

Counselor's Signature

ENCLOSURE (1)

HEALTH CARE PROVIDER PREGNANCY NOTIFICATION TO
COMMANDING OFFICER/OFFICER IN CHARGE (CO/OIC)
FOR OFFICIAL USE ONLY (When Filled In)

Date_____

From: _____

      MTF/Health Care Provider

To: _____

      Commanding Officer/Officer-in-Charge

Subj: _____

      Member's Name

Ref: (a) MCO 5000.12E

1. This is to notify you that a member of your command, _____, is pregnant. Using current dating information, her estimated date of conception is _____. This would make her 20th week about _____ and her 28th week about _____.

2. Please refer to reference (a) which provides current administrative guidance concerning pregnant servicewomen. This guidance is intended to promote uniformity in the medical-administrative management of pregnancies for women in the Marine Corps and assigned to Marine units.

3. Pregnancy is a condition that includes a range of physiological changes that can potentially lead to clinical findings that would result in your command having to modify the servicewoman's job function/working hours. In addition, certain unforeseen conditions related to the pregnancy may arise that could warrant specific medical interaction and further physical limitation of the servicewoman's activities.

_____

      Signature/Rank

ENCLOSURE (2)

Occupational Exposures of Reproductive or Developmental Concern - Worker's Statement

After your supervisor has completed the NAVMED 6260/8, please complete this form and have it with you when you see the health care professional who will help with your evaluation. PLEASE PRINT.

Worker's Name: Last / First / M.I.   SSN: ☐☐☐ - ☐☐ - ☐☐☐☐

Rank/Rate/Job Code: _____   Today's Date: ☐☐ ☐☐ ☐☐☐☐ (Day Month Year)

Age: ___   Sex: ___   Phone (work): _____   Phone (home): _____

Females only

Are you pregnant? ☐ No ☐ Yes   Number of previous pregnancies: ☐

How many were: Live births ☐   Stillbirths ☐   Miscarriages ☐   Abortions ☐

Date last menstrual period began: ☐☐ ☐☐ ☐☐☐☐ (Day Month Year)

Males only

How many children have you fathered (ever)? ☐

All workers

How many years have you had your current job? ☐

What did you do at your previous job? _____

What does your spouse or mate do at work? _____

Have you ever gotten sick or injured because of your job? ☐ No ☐ Yes

Have any of your children had birth defects? ☐ No ☐ Yes

Do you have any illnesses you see the doctor for regularly? ☐ No ☐ Yes

Do you take medications regularly? ☐ No ☐ Yes

Do you use any other drugs, including tobacco? ☐ No ☐ Yes

Give details of any "yes" answers here

How much alcohol do you usually drink per week? ☐ <6 drinks ☐ 6 to 14 ☐ 15 to 21 ☐ 22 or more

Reason for consultation: _____

What reproductive or developmental hazards are you most concerned about? _____

In your activities at home, recreation, hobbies, second job, etc., are you exposed to any of the following? (Check all that apply)

Chemical Agents
☐ Inorganic chemicals
☐ Organic solvents and fuels
☐ Metals - lead, cadmium, etc.
☐ Pesticides
☐ Pharmaceuticals/drugs
☐ Other hazards (specify) _____

Physical Agents
☐ Ionizing radiation
☐ Microwave and other RF radiation
☐ "Noise" (Intense sound)
☐ Thermal stress (heat or cold)
☐ Vibration

Biological Agents
☐ Bacteria   ☐ Animal danders
☐ Fungi   ☐ Endotoxins
☐ Viruses   ☐ Enzymes and other proteins

Physical Conditions
☐ Irregular or shift
☐ Strenuous work

☐ None of the above

_____ Worker's Signature

Occupational Exposures of Reproductive or Developmental Concern - Supervisor's Statement

To be completed by the supervisor for any worker with concerns regarding workplace reproductive or developmental hazards. This form should then be forwarded to appropriate medical personnel such as Occupational Medicine, OB/GYN, etc. Please attach material safety data sheets (MSDS) for any substances to which this worker is exposed.

PLEASE PRINT

Worker's Name _____ _____ ____
                Last   *First*   *M.I.*

SSN ☐☐☐ - ☐☐ - ☐☐☐☐

Rank/Rate/Job Code _____

Date ☐☐ ☐☐ ☐☐☐☐
     Day *Month* *Year*

Supervisor _____

Supervisor's Telephone _____   Worker's Telephone

Command/Shop _____

Job Duties (not job title) _____

Check all boxes that apply

Workplace: ☐ Shipboard ☐ Shop ☐ Office ☐ Outdoors
☐ Other (describe) _____

Is the worker exposed to:

Chemical Agents
☐ Inorganic chemicals
☐ Organic solvents and fuels
☐ Metals - lead, cadmium, mercury, etc. (specify below)
☐ Pesticides (specify below)
☐ Pharmaceuticals/drugs (specify below)
☐ Other hazards (specify below)

Physical Agents
☐ Ionizing radiation
☐ Microwave and other RF radiation
☐ "Noise" (Intense sound)
☐ Thermal stress (heat or cold)
☐ Vibration
☐ Other hazards (specify below)

Biological Agents
☐ Bacteria   ☐ Animal danders
☐ Fungi   ☐ Endotoxins
☐ Viruses   ☐ Enzymes and other proteins
☐ Protozoa   ☐ Other hazards (specify below)

Physical Conditions
☐ Irregular or shift
☐ Strenuous work
☐ Other hazards (specify below)

Specify agents or conditions here

Personal Protective Equipment required:
☐ None ☐ Hearing protection ☐ Gloves
☐ Protective clothing ☐ Respirator

Is the worker in a medical surveillance program?
☐ No ☐ Yes ☐ Don't know

Are there Industrial Hygiene sampling data for the involved worker? ☐ No ☐ Yes

Did the Industrial Hygiene survey reveal reproductive or developmental hazards? ☐ No ☐ Yes (specify)
_____

Has a detailed evaluation of the worksite(s) and/or process(s) with which the worker is involved been performed? ☐ No ☐ Yes

Is the worker required to work shifts? ☐ No ☐ Yes
If yes, which one(s)? _____

Has the worksite had an Industrial Hygiene survey in the last two years?
☐ No ☐ Yes ☐☐ ☐☐ ☐☐☐☐
              Day *Month* *Year*

Has the worker reported an occupational illness or injury in the last year? ☐ No ☐ Yes (specify)
_____

_____
Supervisor's Signature

NAVMED 6260/8 (12-2002)